BLUES JAM
40 PROGRESSIONS AND GROOVES

BY ED FRIEDLAND

T0101728

AUDIO RHYTHM SECTION:

THE COUNTRY BWAHS

ARTHUR MIGLIAZZA - KEYBOARDS

TERRY OUBRE - RHYTHM GUITAR

ED FRIEDLAND - BASS

RALPH GILMORE - DRUMS

To access audio visit:
www.halleonard.com/mylibrary

Enter Code
3105-1597-8076-7180

Cover photo by Peter Amft

ISBN: 978-1-4234-4680-4

HAL•LEONARD®
7777 W. BLUEMOUND RD. P.O. BOX 13819 MILWAUKEE, WI 53213

In Australia contact:
Hal Leonard Australia Pty. Ltd.
4 Lentara Court
Cheltenham, Victoria, 3192 Australia
Email: ausadmin@halleonard.com.au

Visit Hal Leonard Online at
www.halleonard.com

4

Track 1

UPTOWN DOWN

HOWLIN' WOLF

Track 2

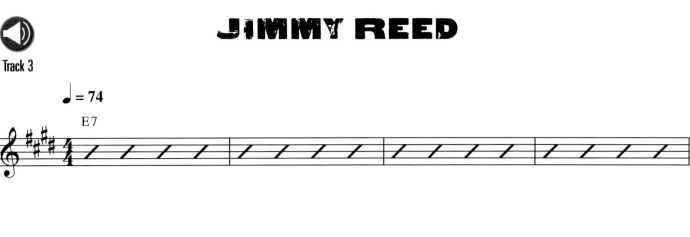

JIMMY REED

♩ = 74

TRAMP

♩ = 100

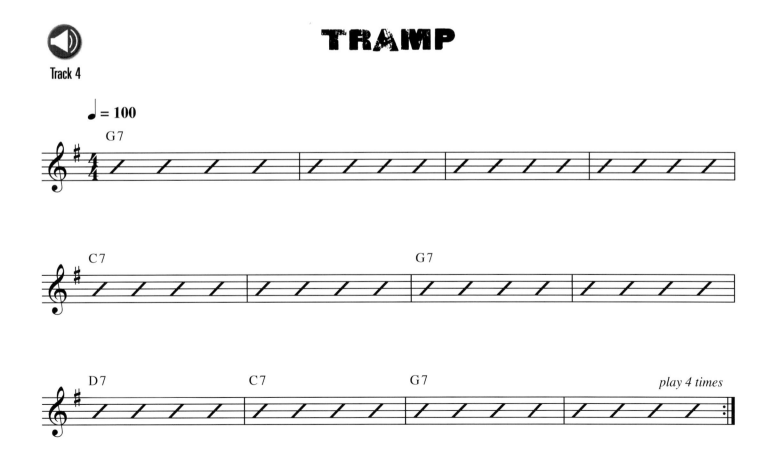

8-BAR SHUFFLE

SLOW T-BONE

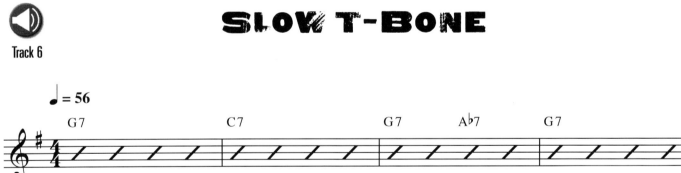

STRAIGHT 8THS

Track 7

 # JUMP BLUES

Track 8

Track 9

MARCH SHUFFLE

♩ = 100

A 7

D 7   A 7

E 7   D 7   A 7   *play 4 times*

Track 10

TEXAS SHUFFLE

♩ = 120

E 7

A 7   E 7

B 7   A 7   E 7   *play 4 times*

FLAT TIRE

Track 11

♩ = 124

FUNKY

Track 12

♩ = 80

10

TEXAS ROCK

Track 13

♩ = 140

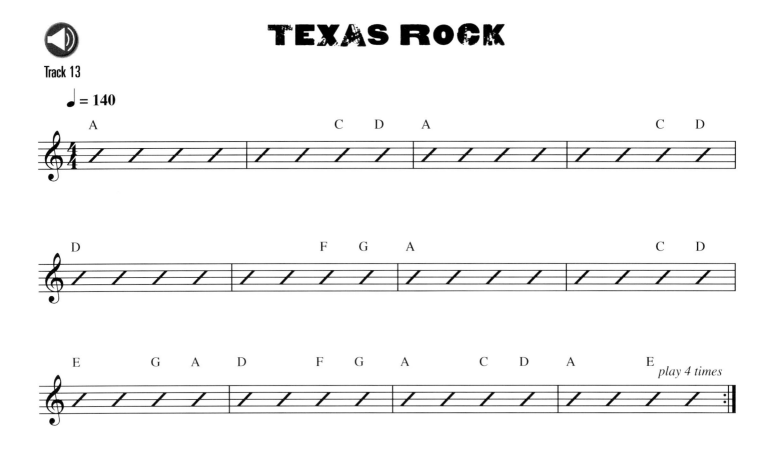

SLOW BLUES

Track 14

♩ = 50

FAST BOOGALOO

Track 15

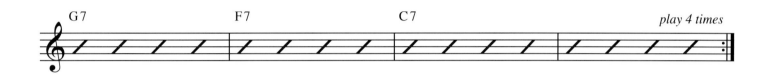

MARCH SHUFFLE #2

Track 16

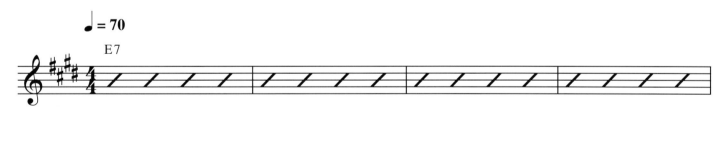

Track 17

FAST FUNKY

Track 18

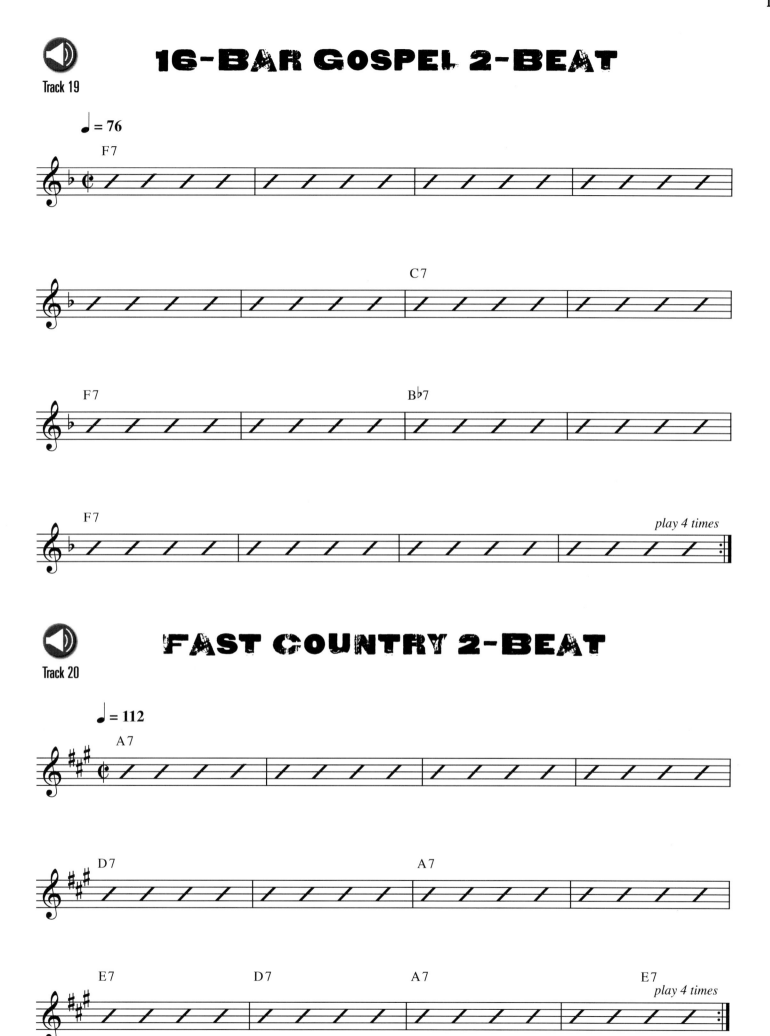

8-BAR SHUFFLE W/BRIDGE

Track 21

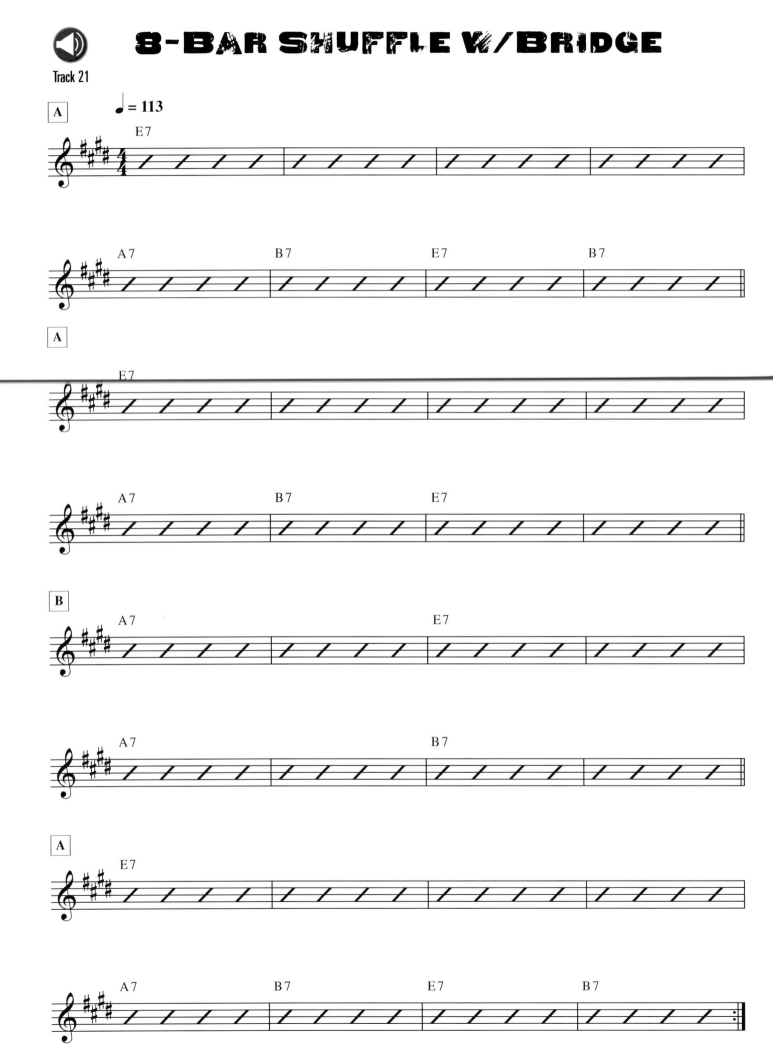

JIMMY REED #2

FUNKY HALF-TIME FEEL

16

JAZZ SWING

♩ = 142

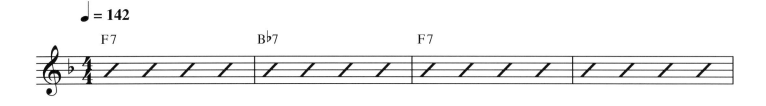

play 5 times

MARCH SHUFFLE #3

♩ = 90

play 4 times

FAST STRAIGHT 8THS

Track 26

$\quad$ = 170

E7

A7 $\qquad$ E7

B7 $\qquad$ E7 $\qquad$ *play 5 times*

NEW ORLEANS FUNK

Track 27

$\quad$ = 76

C7

F7 $\qquad$ C7

G7 $\qquad$ F7 $\qquad$ C7 $\qquad$ *play 3 times*

18

Track 28

AFRO-6/8 FEEL

Track 29

FUNKY BO DIDDLEY

TEXAS SHUFFLE #2

Track 30

BALLAD BLUES

Track 31

TWIST

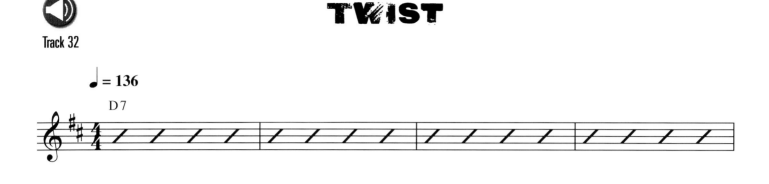

HOOCHIE COOCHIE

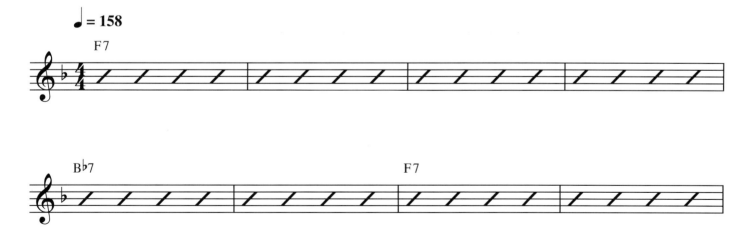

TRAMP #2

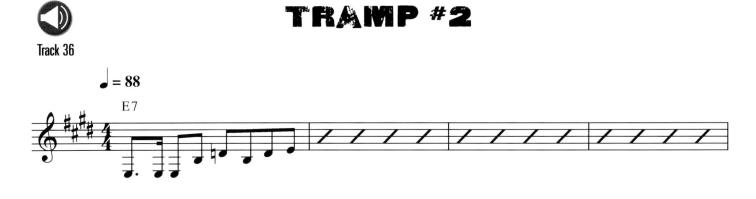

JUMP BLUES #2

8-BAR DIXIELAND

♩ = 126

D 7 · · · · | · · · · | G 7 · · · · | · · · · |

D 7 · · · · | A 7 · · · · | D 7 · · · · | A 7 · · · · | *play 5 times*

FAST JAZZ SWING

♩ = 180

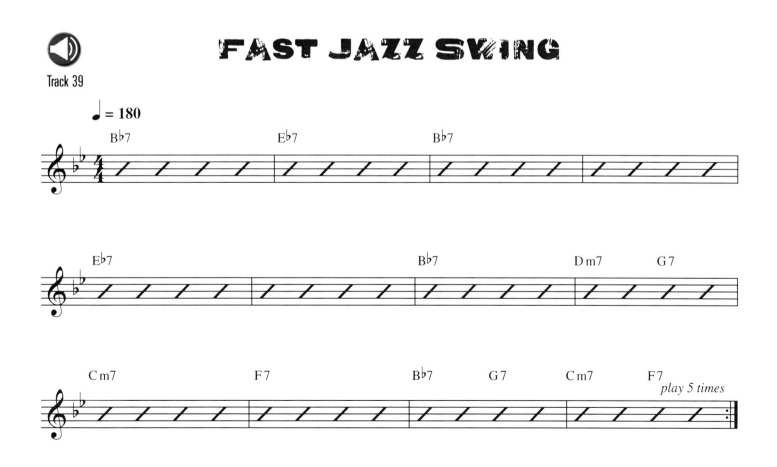

B♭7 · · · · | E♭7 · · · · | B♭7 · · · · | · · · · |

E♭7 · · · · | · · · · | B♭7 · · · · | D m7 · · G 7 · · |

C m7 · · · · | F 7 · · · · | B♭7 · · G 7 · · | C m7 · · F 7 · · | *play 5 times*

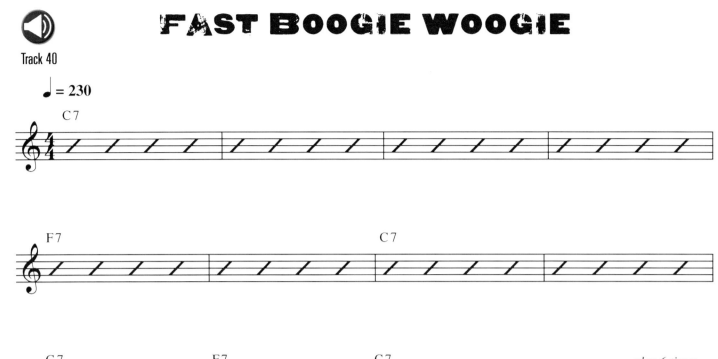

FAST BOOGIE WOOGIE